CHINOI

DEAR READER: WHAT I STARTED TO TELL

SERIE

YOU / HAD SOMETHING TO DO WITH HUNGER

WINNER OF THE
2011 SAWTOOTH POETRY PRIZE

JUDGED BY PAUL HOOVER

❦

AHSAHTA PRESS
BOISE, IDAHO

CHINOISERIE

KAREN RIGBY

Ahsahta Press, Boise State University, Boise, Idaho 83725-1525
http://ahsahtapress.boisestate.edu
http://ahsahtapress.boisestate.edu/books/rigby/rigby.htm
Cover design by Quemadura
Book design by Janet Holmes
Printed in Canada

LIBRARY OF CONGRESS CATALOGING-IN-PUBLICATION DATA

Rigby, Karen.
Chinoiserie / Karen Rigby.
p. cm.
"Winner of the Sawtooth Poetry Prize 2011"— P. [   ].
Includes bibliographical references and index.
ISBN-13: 978-1-934103-25-8 (pbk. : alk. paper)
ISBN-10: 1-934103-25-X (pbk. : alk. paper)
I. Title.
PS3618.I3938C55 2012
811'.6—DC22

2011029409

ACKNOWLEDGMENTS

Grateful acknowledgment is made to the editors of the following publications, where some of these poems first appeared, sometimes in earlier versions: *Anti-*: "Lovers in Anime"; *Arch Literary Journal*: "Love Notes from the Firefly Spanish/English Visual Dictionary"; *Bat City Review*: "Maps We Have Produced in Technicolour"; *Black Warrior Review*: "The Story of Adam and Eve"; *Canteen*: "Greentree Hotel, Pittsburgh"; *Carnegie Mellon Poetry Review*: "Orange/Pittsburgh," "The New York Botanical Garden"; *Carte Blanche*: "Dear Reader"; *Crab Creek Review*: "Bathing in the Burned House"; *failbetter.com*: "Black Roses," "Red Transferware"; *FIELD*: "Knife. Bass. Woman," "Poppies"; *La Fovea*: "Flyover Country"; *Linebreak*: "The Lover"; *Meridian*: "Nightingale & Firebird"; *New England Review*: "Design for a Flying Machine," "New York Song"; *Oak Bend Review*: "After the Bell Has Called the Women from the Fields"; *Phoebe*: "Cebolla Church"; *Quarterly West*: "Red Dress," "Phoenix Nocturne"; *Swink*: "Sleeping on Buses"; *The Straddler*: "Norma Desmond Descending the Staircase as Salome"; *Washington Square*: "In the Lizard-Dark, No Fire in the Orchard." "The Lover" was reprinted in *Best New Poets 2008: 50 Poems from Emerging Writers* (Samovar Press, 2008). "Poppies" was reprinted on *Poetry Daily*, and "Bathing in the Burned House" was reprinted on *Verse Daily*. "Borscht" was reprinted in
O Taste and See: Food Poems (Bottom Dog Press, 2003).

Some of these poems appeared in the chapbooks *Festival Bone* (Adastra Press, 2004) and *Savage Machinery* (Finishing Line Press, 2008).

Thanks also to the National Endowment for the Arts for a 2007 fellowship, to the Vermont Studio Center, and to G. Costanzo, J. Daniels, S. McDermott, G. Metras, J. Huang and family.

CONTENTS

III

PHOENIX NOCTURNE

The skull was never a tomb
or curio. A cage

picked clean

as if bone foretold lessons in turbulence.

Sockets drew you in a masquerade.
            The jaw, which was hinged
                and slack,

                    which was packed cavity,
the cow's head staked to the garden—

Your voice, when it left.
Your voice in the desert
                    circling pink xeriscapes,
radiation lantanas.

The skull anchored at its base
            always *an echo of something else*
                    and when I sought you, wind sheared

cinderblock walls,
when I said *I cannot recall what I started to tell you,*
I meant the pith, bitter-white.

The skull cradled your voice.

You would think that nothing
would ever happen again.

Sirens laced the grid.
Bromegrass silvered in the drained canal.

I

in the canefield of the heart we cross through
a summer of tigers . . .

Pablo Neruda, translated by Donald D. Walsh

DEAR READER

The mink shouldered out of its cage,
paced four meters square.
I admired the indexed spine. The guard hairs
slick. The mouth
suspect.

The black eye trained against the water pump, the white magnolia—
what could I bring to the dooryard?
He wanted nothing of torn bread.
Nothing to drink.

One night the mink climbed my throat
and out of bone and grasping
a demon was born
to haunt the city of steeples.

It blessed the pedestals worn
by thumbprints. Leather Bibles. Rivers bruising
in their beds. Its jaw hung like a petal
darkening by the hour.

Dear reader: What I started to tell you
had something to do with hunger
but the mink was demon
turned bodiless terror.

It led me closer to the firs
where the dead wait for an answer.
All night the mink appeared
and disappeared. The demon wept.

Bodies lined up like blonde guitars
without their necks. Faces I loved thorned
in the trees. A tanager shone
like a pitcher of blood.

NEW YORK SONG

Think of the pear
and its grainy room the color of parchment.

How the weight in your hand
becomes the first song from the grave.
Brother bone, I have knelt

in furious beauty,
drunk root to crown,

loved you in your sleep, and sleeping,
felt your spine
in the shadow of my breasts,

and waking in the first wine
of morning, known the nautilus,

marriage of pearl and roaring.
I know the scent of pepper
and gunmetal,

dark braille my fingers comb.

There is no loneliness
like finned mouths opening on the eve

of something without name.

DESIGN FOR A FLYING MACHINE

Leonardo da Vinci, c. 1488

Nothing but a bridge between
that other life and here, where the stomach of a plane
casts shadows before it burns the acre.
The sketch contains a faceless man, an X
across his chest, the parachute
dreamed centuries too soon,
too late. Early Autumn: leaves
the color of grain. Look at the bat's wing,
brown ink flawed. Each rib
could hold the weight of a balloon
like the one now leaking helium.
Why do we do it, the dumb abandonment?
Houses mushroom in the woods. Imagine the view,
the body speeding in sleep.

POPPIES

Last winter on the corner
of Fifth Avenue paint buckets filled
with poppies. I remember not for their jazz
tearing a backdrop of snow,
but for the way two men unloaded
buds like munitions.

One of them wore fingerless gloves,
cupped cellophane throats.
Below him a brother or son
shuttled fox fur
between the truck
and curb. I knew from the cold kiss

of his touch petals gave no scent—
he did not lean into the red corona, it was
pure commerce. Pods hung,
flammable batteries.

BATHING IN THE BURNED HOUSE

The house shimmers
behind ribbons of heat. Like a child's
shoe-box diorama, three brick walls embrace
the clawfoot tub. Its beveled rim

is painted black. The brass rod
stands upright as a heron.
A woman steps behind the vinyl curtain,

leans toward the spigot.
Drivers touch the ceilings of their cars
when they pass. They think it's lucky
water runs in a burned house.

Women envy her freedom.
Tease husbands, saying church drives
and dry cleaning trips are white lies.
Neighborhood wives

take turns bathing yards
from the road, someone new each week.
Men linger at the curb. Breathe
milled soap, long to be

the sky above the woman's head.
Mid-August, any miracle could surface—
Mary's image graven in the road's peeled tar.

THE STORY OF ADAM AND EVE

Boucicaut Master and Workshop, c. 1415

illuminare

Their spines must have aged
like hooks, those brothers painting
in cold rooms: deep blue
and olive snaking
down a tree. They must have beaten
gold-leaf for each thumbnail,
God pressed in goatskin
every hour. What do I know
about illuminating books, the bowl of saffron
turned to stone? Who remembers
kingfishers on water?

Before the serpent. Before the beasts
lay on their paws, before stones released their heat.
Before the savage machinery.
A woman sprung from bone facing her husband,
his body inside her, his body a wing
in thickened amber—

—as in the riffling surface
        of things revealed. As in the palm turned
            to the word flensed
                from the body of God,

as in the first breath murmured in the man's lungs
and how I understood
when the city blacked out

and substations powered off,
sudden downpour
at midday, women in voile skirts
clinging like seaweed—

In fifteenth-century Paris
the manuscript inked with quills
cut from a swan
becomes a measure
of the will, but also of the vine.

About the beginning
I could tell you the garden bloomed
multiple bells. I could say
everything I know about beauty I learned
from the body's ruin:
the rib drawn
through his quartered skin,
the skin sewn and the woman born,
a dark homunculus.

I could listen
for the first rasp like the hinge
on a storm door and I would know
the beginning was the word, but also the soot.
Also the lie.

Think of the parchmenter scraping

his curved blade

cutting double-leaves   soaked in lime

Think of the calligrapher

gesso   lamp-black   oak gall   mineral pigments

the book revealing what *bereft* means:

field whelmed with salt

crows echoing their brothers the songbirds

city of exiles given to powdered iron.

ORANGE/PITTSBURGH

Robins pulse at their feeders—
Chinese bottle gourds
strung along the black elm.

Downtown, a canyon
of brick & avenue
moves toward the river,

water folds over pockets
of walleye. Orange is girder
& rusted flange, citrine

in the Orr's gemcase.
DETOUR. Milk crate.
The molten globe

on a glassblower's rod.
Every morning, the muscular
hum & hand-over-hand:

ropes tensing on the pier.
Orange is Japanese carp
beneath the tattoo needle,

habaneros sweating
in their grocery bins.
French horns warming

on the south cathedral lawn.
Every morning flames rise
over columns sandblasted clean.

FLYOVER COUNTRY

Pittsburgh to Midway, Midway to Phoenix,
               redeye you took last winter, the couple
beside you sleeping, together   but separate

in their dark circling, like skaters
        on Breughel's platinum lake, then a memory

         of mannequins suspended
in neon aquariums—

        their eyes like the unwavering eyes on totems.
Fiberglass breasts. Cityscapes melting

to suburbs, fields, saguaros. The year the neighborhood
       burned Christmas trees in January,

       no one would haul the branches
with their clean, medicinal scent.

Buildings burned on TV. You remembered spires
       stripped of their silver:
                    a parable for loneliness.

       Fences chalked with moonlight.
Grooves worn by a car's tires.

Whatever you lived then, east of the Mississippi,
       whatever you know now, the plane a red thorn

in the century's gaslight.

NIGHTINGALE & FIREBIRD

As if the song encoded in the wheel could railroad
to the garden, the mechanical grind transformed

the nightingale to music-box, the music to evergreen
vistas. The firebird was another story: inventory

of dust on the wings. Dried blood on the red-gold
coat. One thread about tin substitutes for splendor,

the other a ghost-image for your burdened heart.
Easy to confuse the black chinoiserie with feathers

torn from ashes, twin halves for a childhood fear:
you were never loved. You could surrender

to the hammer or the flame but no one would come.
That which they called *wonder* was only a greased key

in a courtesan's palm, and when the bird sang, no one
heard the sound a wing makes when the current breaks.

CEBOLLA CHURCH

Georgia O'Keeffe, 1945

The desert is a lion-colored seam.

Not a finger of dust lines sills—
not a spine or lizard scale.

It could be any thumb-shaped blur
against the window pane:

sexton. Thief.

Before villagers bring stems
sliced beneath cold faucets,

someone has to sweep.
Someone lights the long, pitched room

like the hold of a ship,
stacks books beneath each bench.

Because the face held
by the hand recedes,

it could be the soul itself
gazing out of the Santo Niño church,

beyond clay erasures.

One month, news kept looping
the same reel of the last wreck.

Men roamed like beekeepers
in their white suits.

I pictured walls radiating gold—
the church with its slant door.

Someone listening
for a distant thundering.

II

But forgetfulness does not exist, dreams do not exist;
flesh exists.

Federico García Lorca, translated by Robert Bly

KNIFE. BASS. WOMAN.

The wood handle thick
as a cattail. Two pegs the color of pewter
anchor the blade. In my left hand,
the knife. Eggs balance on the tip.
The bass hangs, its zippery spine
loose. Each stroke brings down
a host of scales. Skin rolls
like hose. Over soaked paper
I understand why a man rapes
before dawn: for the red-rimmed eye,
fearful and waiting. For the puff
of cheek, air catching
her throat. The woman on Vine
wore flannel. Maybe her skin smelled
like pilings near the water's edge—
wood-rot, sweet. I wonder
what book she thumbed, what kept
the lightbulb burning. A man carries
sperm like a black suitcase.

THE LOVER

A film by Jean-Jacques Annaud, 1992 / Marguerite Duras, *The Lover* (tr. Barbara Bray)

The shuttered room a mind's throw
from the truant girl flashing sequined heels

linen and lipstick   oxcarts

                fried bread

                    the Chinese district

     her body as shorthand
     for what his body mistook for love—

you knew the lovers would fail but nothing stops
     the double-timed insouciance

                  leaving mother and brothers
   a blindsight   the plantation

hammered to its slant foundation.

The victrola's fox trot one more static to bear.

                       ❧

Because hunger traced the Mekong.
Because water broke
     the salt-row harvest.

Because wind fluttered the girl's neckline

Indochina minted on your tongue.

Marguerite Duras wrote *there are no seasons in that part of the world . . .*
no spring, no renewal

       no sound for the girl's hand releasing the rail,
the ferry an image you held in that humid air.

Fortune.   Fever.

The lover twice her age. In the colony
                unthinkable

                this.

The alley patterned the wall in submarine blooms.

The girl returned
               root-bound
                      to the bachelor's room,
       her body betraying its grammar,
bone rose, notched zero.

1929 Saigon
rehearsed the girl

for the canopy viewed
from the footbridge:

his wedding
silk brocade.

❧

Whiffs of burnt sugar drift
into the room, the smell of roasted peanuts,
Chinese soups, roast meat,

herbs, jasmine, dust, incense, charcoal fires,
they carry fire
about in baskets here

it's sold in the street, the smell of the city
is the smell of the villages
upcountry, of the forest . . .

❧

Marguerite was the French girl
writing the snaked road / scent swarming /
limbs slickened with resins / the lover raising
a palmful of water / after love
you enter and leave / you leave writing
it was already too late.

❧

Out of lung sacs.
Out of blood. Mosquito nets.
Out of mornings in Sa Dec
       the glamour of the girl
             grew separate from the house
                flooded with voices

the river's clockwork   sunburned trees
the scissors inside her singing *the sea, the immensity* . . .

LOVERS IN ANIME

1.]   couple on elevated trains. In hot springs. Libraries.
Apartments lit by the Ferris wheel on the plaza.

2.]   Sakuras splice with birds alighting: a montage
of petals and a round-mouthed *O*.

3.]   The person you loved will lead you
to Hamada City or the bamboo
whitened by snow.

4.]   Windchimes remind you of the shore.

5.]   Simple equations, but also the way a girl's pink hair
satins through your palm.

6.]   Places you meet turn semaphore:
the tree a shrine blackened by fire.

7.]   Women as half-demons/half-gods.
School festivals. Texture of red bean paste.

8.]   Swords hidden in a tea-length dress.

9.]   If one of you bears witness, the other will haul
you back from the precipice.

10.]   Vending machine tea solves nothing,
but treat it like a balm.

11.]   For every azalea or water wheel, every courtyard,
        every alley crosshatched, someone waits
        to *confess*.

12.]   The Golden Mean does not apply to bodies.
        Eyes span larger distances and breasts point perpendicular
        to the ground.

13.]   Train copper strips around pine: bonsai
        grow in glazed ceramic.

14.]   Hoshino. Yumi. Aiko. Whatever your name,
        only the suffix (*-san* or *-chan*) matters
        on a lover's tongue.

15.]   If you never admit it, the one you love
        loves someone else who loves the person that loves
        you back.

16.]   Ground you claim, cutting sunburned weeds,
        divining patterns on the smooth backs of stones—

17.]   Storm drain clouding with letters.

18.]   Graduation: swift bravura, heel turns.
        The talcum odor.

19.]   Something trails out of limelight. The violin strums.

RED DRESS

                        Because handkerchief hems
            jag like tropicals blown
                        against the breakwater,

            every woman has read
            scandal in a red dress. Because the body hums
            that armor. Because red announces
            a lone hibiscus
                        behind Rita Hayworth's ear,

            choose the strapless number: rayon shirred
            from the center of your breasts.
            Red *llantos*. String knotted
            on a lover's wrist.

            Red lotteries, accordions, *telenovelas*
            flickering emergencies.
            Red you bitch-heel
                        past avenues humid as horses
                            rounding a wet track,
            red name traced on mirrors:
            amor, whose vowels betray me.

            Red dress of apocalypse.
            Red tangos. Bertolucci's Isabelle
            thumbing the jukebox, dreaming Dietrich
            and Joplin, civil unrest.

A woman's carriage from the waist-up.
The belly-dance hotter than shaved
magnesium. Choose red for hubris—
               barbell pierced
                        through your lip—
susurrando like fists.

PHOTO OF AN AUTOEROTIC

After the first shock, you have to
admire the body's hardwood cursive.

His face
        concealing his member,
                            his thumb
and forefinger
        hooking his head

to his own lip like a snake charmer,
        something fabled but true:

the ones bowing to kiss themselves,
        holding the pose for the shutter,

                the aluminum flash.

You remember the song
                composed of gestures
        for the mute tongue.

The hand a salt cellar, compass,
        pharmacy
                for the struck mouth.

The scent reminds you of pennies
        greening underwater

and the boy whose mother told him
      not to bear

someone else's   wishes home.
Everywhere in this city doorways lit

            by argon lights   remind you

                  there are rooms behind
the ones you know.

            Already the boy is learning
to let go: a matchbook

                  missing half its lashes,
the queen wasp dormant in the window frame.

SLEEPING ON BUSES

How does she manage, the woman on Forbes,
so sure no one stretching for the cord
will stroke her face, a gesture saved for the dying
or women caught in stairwells, that faint
apology for love? How does she know
when slate roofs turn to poplars
where the Greek church burned?
The woman breathes, no one to signal home.
She listens for her street the way the blind
count closing doors. In the black Monongahela,
bottomfish lie perfect in their element.

MAPS WE HAVE PRODUCED IN TECHNICOLOUR

Splendor in the Grass, directed by Elia Kazan

Of sirens spliced in reels, voices brandied in the defunct dramas—
pave the prairie with expectation, but oil runs furthest
from the road you thumb back.

⸎

Suicides that weren't.
Suicides that were.

1929 blowing ticker-tape.
The bottle spitting its cork

like a derrick so you can't miss
the obvious symbol.

Whichever girl you follow
to the parked car, the scent

of Pears something to save,
something to breach.

⸎

Deanie swimming the bluffs is a plumb-line
between the ground and sky: gin funneling heat.
Her red dress a technicolour roadmap
and mother asking whether she'd been good
when *good* meant inflorescense without bees.

The heart equivocates madness: beasts
in their public rooms. An animal odor on her tongue.

Everything feral seizes
in the brain. The yellow corridor.

A deer at the edge
of a banked road. The barbed-wire-thought
she could drown

in that house with its walnut highboy,
ceramic pitchers chilled beside each bed.

Deanie cuts hair to her chin.

Thereafter, every act
some witchery signaling the nerves.

Otherwise, there is no story.
Mother and father arguing, the coffee
a black lake between them.

Against the cellar door the rain, the threat
of rain, the drumbeat for the lettered boy,
as when a kiss slides past your ear.

꧅

When the body bent like brushwork,
quarter-notes beat against the reservoir.

꧅

You could build an ark of curios
from women crushing pills

for pain, speak nothing of water
            constellating wound
                        or bruised skin,
                                    sea-faring stink.

꧅

You survive (the windswept dogwood).

You return to the wide-brimmed Kansas afternoon
(better to have never ravaged)

the one tour-de-force of your life—

(the rotary   the mouth-box   voluble)

some fever to asylum——

GREENTREE HOTEL, PITTSBURGH

The bolt joining the strike plate.

Hair wound through a boar's brush, sounds we make
                as if driven to watch

each other's rituals

but it never happens   we never sleep
                in that city tattooed

with verdigris. We never sleep
                but sex after long absence.

We drink the neighborhood scent—

                sourwood   catalpa   honeylocust

                we drink to the body's ligatures.

We drink to forget
                we almost died,
                        but lived,
                                as one does.

Outside the Carnegie musuem a bronze dinosaur
                hangs above traffic.

Joggers wind beyond the conservatory road, steam rising
above them.

We never sleep but edge against each other's skin.

We thieve the hour before a pitchful
of earth on fire.

AFTER THE BELL HAS CALLED THE WOMEN FROM THE FIELDS

Brewed in tinctures.

Sewn in sachets.

Nailed from lintels

upside down to dry,

crimped blooms

permeate like camphor

or green hay.

All summer stems

turn slantwise

like serrated knives.

Wind carries

low notes

through lavender

aisles. The iron bell

calls women

to *lavandula* steaming.

At nightfall, traces

of woodsmoke.

Women draw water

in pairs, ladle broth

in lion-head tureens,

but no one remembers

before the distillery

and blue bottles, volatile oil.

What if the field

were flight path?

Screen memory?

A dress opens like the field,

which was rent,

divided in fingers eastward.

Indigo fireworks

sear the edge of the village.

A midwife's tale:

women sleep

through brilliancies.

Plentitude skimmed

beneath their palms.

After the bell, women

leopard into eves.

DARK HORSE

To be the dark horse,
pummel raked conclusions,

        inhale
              riderless—

engine groomed
        from nothing—

thief of your good name

that I might reside
among legends

and lavish gestures: rose grazing
the ice rink. The hearse

        searing roadways
to gangplanks.

To be the gun like a water hammer.
Hoard sevens and snake eyes.

Do one exceptional thing,
which was justice

        in the last shall be first,
windburn through the blind swerve.

The paddock vacant of hoofprints
and the gate sprung clear

of hornets and gorse fields—

I waited all my life
for the dry track,

the streetfight brutal with gold.

LOVE NOTES FROM THE FIREFLY
SPANISH/ENGLISH VISUAL DICTIONARY

When you find me in the courtyard
of a Roman home, bring seven legumes,
a turbine, the cross-section

of a stone fruit, and a white fennec.
Strike the soundboard and the dance
is an olive grove pitted with light.

Cross the hangar and the index
for zeppelin parts could diagram
pork cuts: patchwork viewed

from 35,000 feet up. In the chapter
on chemistry, we siphon potions
in milligrams. On p. 537, the bait-

casting reel resembles a music-box.
Names for the kingdom, monorails,
arthropods—the ocean spits *buccino*

for good luck. We kiss in thickets
of serifs. Have I mentioned that I love
your eye, and its anterior chamber?

At moonrise, tikis light generals
on plinths. We brace for cartoon
weather toasting guava juice coolers.

Tugboats dock in housewares.
We aim for greener *cordilleras*,
the republic gunning our backs.

PLUMS

Friars. Red beauties. Elephant hearts
you could pare on your tongue, limbs darkening
below the line. Between each load
of shirts pinned sleeve to sleeve,
you'd raise the basket,
bend among the trees.
Some of the plums tightened
like a baby's fist. You pricked their skins,
packed buckets with sugar and lemon.
Six trays dried on the long bench.
All evening fireflies
haunted you with syncopations,
and when you came to the Santa Rosas,
the fruit of the spirit was patient as knives
sharpened with pumice. Forget what you know.
What should he bring to your hunger
if not his own wrist?

III

What sustains it,
half-open, the clarity of nightfall,
the light let loose in the gardens?

Octavio Paz, translated by Eliot Weinberger

BLACK ROSES

None. Only burgundy or violet,
scene you never imagine,
fields burning with larvicide.

Black Magic, Lavaglut,
Ruby Celebration, holy grail
of botany furled like ironwork.

Not even carnations
split along their stems
to drink the florist's dye

approach the order of the rose.
Some say petals scorch
easily, the symbol turned

Vampiric: floribundas
staked from Syria to parlors
of the Art Nouveau.

Always a rose entwined
with rose, given in ardor
or vengeance. Kiss-of-death.

Blood-of-martyrs. Novel.
Noir. *Baccara, Barkarole.*
Black rose dried in vellum,

black rose frosted in nitrogen,
black rose tattooed, genus
prized for being almost true.

Essence of dream. Apothecary.
How I loved you, whittling
thorns, loved you not.

RED TRANSFERWARE

The pagoda's roof curls beyond a lake-view glazed
in reproduction pink on serveware matched to the
butter dish, the gravy boat, the once-a-year feast—no
Villeroy & Boch, but good enough, *herr doktor*, to fake
that recherché look. Pastorals stand for the village, and
candles, like black trees in the Brothers Grimm, script
happiness we could drown in.

                Ladies inked on ironstone
sleep the sleep of the dead. We hear their hearts clink
        with elegant thrift. We hear their forks tuned
                      to another orbit.

The foxhole
with its grass selvage
limns a hunger
thin as bleeding-edge prints.

White rose, red ranunculus.
      Red rose, ganglion of wires.
           White asparagus, red coulis, cool arrangements,
dinners like driftwood in the ark of *hospitable*:
      surfeits of terror and pleasure.

Before the first snow, before the last course,
maleficium settles in our lungs. We swallow bitter
like good guests. The red line
hems our plates.

❧

Of bindweed or fluorishes, nothing to say about the hand's elaboration.
Of creamware, only stacked and brittle confusion.

We bargain daylight out of black bread.

❧

1756:   Copper etched with scenes from Britannia or East Asia.
         Manors and pheasants. Peppercorn-prints.

2010:   Where nothing had lived we built an altar of porticos.

Set the cows in good stead against the beadboard hutch /
paperwhites / ginger jar / cake plate.

❧

Josiah Spode: what crockery
                      what England
                      what codex drawn
                      in scalloped borders?

Red tide nothing like Hokusai.

The house weathers an eye
                    that won't rest.

                              ✎

Scoured with salt and lemon
the tea stain dissipates.

We set the table with transferware.
Pretended women could speak.

When the willow swept past us,
no summons,
no cyclone
but *this*—

IN THE LIZARD-DARK, NO FIRE IN THE ORCHARD

In the lizard-dark, no fire in the orchard.
No moonlight. Nothing but a blue hoop turned
along the horizon, the street

a white pastoral
framed in the after-image.

Everything remains: decanters pouring
no wine. The wedding mantled in blue.
The grim pandemic

painted in poison chromatics.
If I think of music,
                        it's not the snow
blown through the artist's skull, nor bergamot
crushed in its mortar. Not the slap

of double-dutch. Children's marble games.
Nights the mariners return—
hands carved
                        against the carapace.
It is the Flemish harbor mantled
around us. Panic of blood-rise, village of blue.

NORMA DESMOND DESCENDING
THE STAIRCASE AS SALOME

Sunset Boulevard, 1950

The heart's declensions beat against
the newsreel storm. The beaded shawl
ropes through my arms. The script

would have you believe grief muscled
into me: asked for, and given the head
of a saint. When the klieg lights sear

my skin I don't remember the body
bloating in the pool or the Black Maria
nosing down my drive. I don't remember

when I shot Joe Gillis—only the blue
flute singing. I could live forever
raising my own hand to my neck,

each time surprised by its cool pulse.
In that kohl-rimmed prime
I calculate seductions stair by stair.

Between the keyless rooms and the city
that loved me no one speaks as if
my crossing were the deposition

of a god. Blood winters in my veins.
The hammered air burns lonely
as bones turning in sleep.

BORSCHT

Throw a bone in the crock.
Cut onions, bon-voyage streamers,
rub tendons with marjoram

and cabbage soft enough to tear
on my tongue. Give me
the good stink of root cellar

and white night, soup so crimson
I could paint the walls:
blood from the mink farms,

hands riveting bolts
to the gunwale of a ship.
Public beatings in Yevtushenko's

Babi Yar. Borscht steams
like a horse combed to a rich gloss
for the May Day parade.

Once, on a tour of Orthodox domes,
a bicyclist rode past balancing
his green gardener's pail

between the handlebars.
Potatos and a newborn dog
bedded on newsprint.

The man could hardly steer
with the weight of his gifts.
Country of exiles, bath houses,

blood of czars—
I raise the bowl and drink
to the steppe's red beets.

LELOUCH LAMPEROUGE PILOTS THE KNIGHTMARE

Code Geass: Lelouch of the Rebellion

Clearing a bluff, an 11 warehouse,
one hook of the wired arm
and you inside the blue manifold
decoding signs:
your brother
against you, the empire
against you, the same as any teenage boy
except for the eye,
the gaze transfiguring desire.

When you were rapt, a thrum in the ribcage.
When you vectored quadrants as Zero of the Order of the Black Knights,
a forest illumined: the hunted at rest.
The hunter lowering his gunsight.

All points lead
to Shinjuku ghetto.
The mask a fencer's grid.
The cloak a lepidopterist's dream.
No end to your double life.
No god in the machine.
No leafage to lay it down by:
your mother bulleted. Imperial siege.

Death comes in the guise
of a robot migration
the color of wolves turned inside out.

THE NEW YORK BOTANICAL GARDEN

The audio tour explains harvesting
palm hearts. Outside, hoarfrost burns the lawn.
I'm inside the snow-globed conservatory peering into
a replica hut: hammock slung
from a beam, mortar and pestle
stationed on the floor. Placards label
everything like a crime. Tell me
something new about the manicole acreage.
A human organ salvaged from the wreck,
my own heart tinned.

NOTES

Forbes is one of the main avenues in Pittsburgh, Pennsylvania.

Isabelle is one of the characters in Bernardo Bertolucci's 2003 film *The Dreamers*.

The title "After the Bell Has Called the Women from the Fields" is a line from Quan Barry's poem "Post-partum" (*Asylum*, University of Pittsburgh Press, © 2001).

Lelouch Lamperouge is a character in *Code Geass: Lelouch of the Rebellion,* an anime written by Ichirō Ōkouchi.

ABOUT THE AUTHOR

KAREN RIGBY is the author of the chapbooks *Savage Machinery* (2008) and *Festival Bone* (2004). A National Endowment for the Arts literature fellow and past resident at the Vermont Studio Center, she has been published in *Washington Square*, *Black Warrior Review*, *Best New Poets 2008*, and other journals. She is a cofounder of *Cerise Press*, and a member of the National Book Critics Circle.

AHSAHTA PRESS

SAWTOOTH POETRY PRIZE SERIES

2002: Aaron McCollough, *Welkin* (Brenda Hillman, judge)

2003: Graham Foust, *Leave the Room to Itself* (Joe Wenderoth, judge)

2004: Noah Eli Gordon, *The Area of Sound Called the Subtone* (Claudia Rankine, judge)

2005: Karla Kelsey, *Knowledge, Forms, The Aviary* (Carolyn Forché, judge)

2006: Paige Ackerson-Kiely, *In No One's Land* (D. A. Powell, judge)

2007: Rusty Morrison, *the true keeps calm biding its story* (Peter Gizzi, judge)

2008: Barbara Maloutas, *the whole Marie* (C. D. Wright, judge)

2009: Julie Carr, *100 Notes on Violence* (Rae Armantrout, judge)

2010: James Meetze, *Dayglo* (Terrance Hayes, judge)

2011: Karen Rigby, *Chinoiserie* (Paul Hoover, judge)

AHSAHTA PRESS

NEW SERIES

This book is set in Apollo MT type
with OPTI Corvinus and Perpetua Titling MT titles
by Ahsahta Press at Boise State University
Cover design by Quemadura
Book design by Janet Holmes

AHSAHTA PRESS

2012

JANET HOLMES, DIRECTOR

JODI CHILSON, MANAGING EDITOR

KYLE CRAWFORD

CHARLES GABEL

KATE HOLLAND

WALLY HUMPHRIES

TORIN JENSEN

JESSICA JOHNSON, *intern*

GENNA KOHLHARDT

JULIE STRAND

JASON STEPHENS, *intern*

MATT TRUSLOW

ZACH VESPER

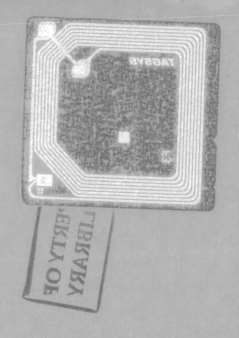